Contents

Chapter 1: Your Niche

Carving a Path

In the ever-expanding online marketplace, it's not just about what you sell, but how uniquely you sell it. Identifying your niche, that special area where your craft stands out, is the cornerstone of turning your hobby into a successful online business.

Being a jack-of-all-trades in the craft world can sometimes mean mastering none. When you attempt to cater to everyone, you often end up resonating with no one. A niche narrows your focus, allowing you to perfect your craft, tailor your marketing, and cater to a specific audience segment. This reduced competition means your products are more likely to be seen, appreciated, and purchased by those actively seeking them.

1. The Importance of Niche Markets

The world of crafts is as vast and varied as the artisans who contribute to it. From intricate beadwork to hand-carved furniture, the online market is flooded with talent. So, how do you ensure that your crafted creations don't just become a needle in this vast haystack? The answer lies in specialisation: finding a niche.

A niche market is a specific segment of a larger market that caters to a particular kind of customer or product. Focusing on a niche does two things for you:

Reduces Competition: Instead of competing with thousands of general crafters, you cater to a specific group, making your products stand out.

Builds Expertise: Specialising in a particular craft or product type allows you to hone your skills, increasing the quality and value of your work over time. Consistency breeds mastery.

Loyal Customer Base: People love brands who 'get them'. When you cater to a niche you're essentially saying, "I see you, and I've created this just for you". This fosters loyalty, repeat buyers and eventually ambassadors for your craft.

2. Exploring Different Crafts and Their Demand

Before you pinpoint your niche, take a moment to explore the vast world of crafts. As you are reading this book I will assume you have a craft in mind already. Some high level categories include:

Traditional Crafts: Think of quilting, knitting, and pottery. These crafts have stood the test of time and have dedicated audiences.

Digital Crafts: With the rise of technology, digital artwork, designs, and even digital scrapbooking has found its place in the craft market.

Eco-friendly Crafts: As the world becomes more environmentally conscious, crafts made from sustainable materials or upcycled goods have seen a surge in popularity.

Cultural or Regional Crafts: Crafts that represent specific cultures or regions, like Native American beadwork or Japanese Origami, can appeal to specific audiences or those looking for authentic cultural items.

To identify the demand for different crafts, tools like Google Trends, Etsy's Trending Items, or Pinterest's trending section can offer insights into what craft enthusiasts are currently seeking.

3. 5 Steps to Identify Your Unique Craft Niche

Finding your niche is like finding your voice in the vast choir of crafters. Here's a step-by-step guide to help you:

Self-Reflection: What are you most passionate about? What craft can you lose yourself in for hours? Start there. List down the crafts that you genuinely enjoy, the skills you excel in and the projects you've received compliments on. This is your foundation.
Consider where you see yourself in the future, mass production or personalised high value crafts?

Is there a specific principle you stand by, like sustainability or cultural representation?

Research: Look into online marketplaces and see what's oversaturated and where there might be gaps you can fill. You can identify top sellers in categories you're interested in and study the price range and reviews. It is also good to enter forums and blogs to keep ahead of trends.

Feedback: Share your work with friends, family, or craft communities, and gauge their responses. They might see a niche appeal in your work that you hadn't noticed. Be open to criticism.

Test the Waters: Before fully diving in, try selling a few items in your chosen niche. See how the audience responds. You can do this online short term, Facebook market place or even direct to friends. Craft fairs are also a good option.

Iterate: Your first choice might not be the final one. It's okay to evolve your niche as you grow and learn more about the market. Stay adaptable and open to learning. You may notice a weak point in your skills, or a shift in market demand. You can bridge skill gaps through workshops, webinars, classes or even just good old fashioned YouTube.

By the end of this process, you'll hopefully have a clearer idea of where your craft fits in the digital marketplace. Remember, in the world of online crafts, sometimes it's the quirkiest, most unique items that catch the eye and heart of the buyer. Your niche is your strength; it's where your passion meets the world's demand. Embrace it, and you'll be well on your way to turning your hobby into a lucrative online venture.

Chapter 2: Setting Up Shop Online

The digital realm is rife with opportunities for craft sellers to showcase and sell their unique creations. Yet, the variety of platforms can make the initial setup seem daunting. In this chapter, we'll delve deep into the nuances of different online platforms tailored for craft sellers, weighing their pros and cons, and guiding you through the initial steps to make your digital debut.

Overview of Online Platforms for Craft Sellers

 A specialised marketplace for handmade items, vintage goods, and craft supplies. Etsy thrives on its community-oriented approach and offers an extensive, built-in customer base keen on unique, handcrafted products.

Pros:
- User-friendly interface suitable for beginners.
- Established trust among consumers seeking handcrafted products.
- Low startup cost.

Cons:
- Competition can be fierce due to a large number of sellers.
- Fees include a listing fee, transaction fee, and payment processing fee.
- Less control over branding and customer experience.

Registration:
- Free to open a shop but has listing fees.
- Fees: Includes a listing fee ($0.20 per item), a 5% transaction fee, and a 3% + $0.25 payment processing fee.
- Basics: Sellers need to provide a valid credit card and bank account for transactions. Items should be handmade, vintage, or craft supplies.

A handcrafted section within the giant e-commerce platform, Amazon. It offers artisans a vast audience, riding on the established trust and reach of the Amazon brand.

Pros:
- Access to a massive customer base of Amazon.
- Trust associated with the Amazon brand.
- Prime eligibility can boost sales.

Cons:
- Higher fees compared to other platforms.
- Strict guidelines and quality checks.
- Less personalization for sellers.

Registration:
- Requires an application to ensure products are handcrafted.
- Fees: 15% referral fee (min $1) on the sale price (including gift wrap and excluding sales tax).
- Basics: Artisans must ensure all products are handmade by them or their employees. Machine-made products require special approval.

Unlike Etsy or Amazon Handmade which are marketplaces, Shopify allows you to set up your standalone online store. It provides a host of customization features and integrative tools, making it a suitable choice for craft sellers envisioning long-term growth and brand establishment.

Pros:
- Complete control over branding and design.
- Access to a vast array of plugins and integrative tools.
- Potential to scale the business.

Cons:
- Monthly subscription fees.
- Might require some technical know-how for customization.
- No built-in audience; relies heavily on your marketing efforts.

Registration:
- Offers a 14-day free trial, after which you choose a subscription plan.
- Fees: Monthly fees range from $29 to $299, plus credit card rates and potential additional fees for certain features or apps.
- Basics:Custom domain name, set up product listings, and design your storefront. No restrictions on the nature of products, but they must adhere to Shopify's terms of service.

There are numerous other platforms like Big Cartel, WooCommerce (for WordPress users), and Storenvy, each offering varied features catering to different needs.

Selecting the right platform to set up your online craft shop is pivotal in your journey from craft hobbyist to entrepreneur. Each platform has its distinct advantages and limitations. By aligning your business goals, budget, and vision with the platform's offerings, you can lay a strong foundation for your online craft enterprise.

Chapter 3: Branding and Presentation

As you venture into the online world of crafts, remember that your digital store is more than just a selling space—it's an extension of your identity. While the quality of your crafts remains paramount, the manner in which you present them is equally vital. Branding isn't just about a logo or a catchy name; it's about crafting a narrative and evoking emotions that make your craft stand out in the vast digital marketplace.

The Importance of Branding in Online Sales

In the vast digital marketplace, where customers are flooded with choices at every click, a memorable brand can be the beacon that draws their attention. The impact of branding transcends beyond mere aesthetics; it is a powerful tool that weaves a narrative, establishes credibility, and fosters loyalty. Branding is crucial for online sales, especially in the craft domain.

1. Setting the Tone for Customer Expectations

A Visual Introduction: Before a potential customer reads a product description or browses your shop, they first see your brand's visuals. This creates an instantaneous perception, setting expectations regarding the quality, style, and ethos of your products.

Narrating a Story: Every element of your brand, from colour schemes to logos, tells a story. It subtly communicates the essence of your craft, the inspiration behind it, and your dedication to the art form.

2. Building Trust and Credibility

Consistency is Key: Consistent branding across product listings, social media, and packaging signals professionalism. It assures customers that you pay attention to detail and are serious about your craft.

Assurance of Quality: A well-thought-out brand indicates investment—both in time and resources. This often translates in customers' minds as a commitment to quality and reliability.

Familiarity Breeds Comfort: Recognisable branding can make repeat customers feel at home. Familiarity is comforting and can instil a sense of trust in your audience.

3. Fostering Emotional Connections

Beyond Transactions: Branding has the power to convert simple transactions into experiences. When customers feel connected to a brand's story or ethos, they're more likely to engage, return, and even advocate for the brand. Written messages in the delivery package or a signature extra helps solidify the brand feel.

Evoking Emotions: Effective branding can evoke specific emotions. For instance, earthy tones might evoke feelings of warmth and authenticity, while a minimalist design might convey sophistication and elegance.

Relatability: Sharing your journey, inspirations, and challenges through branding can make your brand relatable. It becomes less of a faceless online shop and more of a passionate artist sharing their craft with the world.

4. Differentiating in a Saturated Market

Standing Out: Especially in popular craft categories, there might be hundreds, if not thousands, of sellers offering similar products. Strong branding can make you stand out in this sea of sameness.

Highlighting USP: Your Unique Selling Proposition (USP) can be accentuated through branding. Be it your sustainable crafting methods, a particular cultural influence, or innovative designs—branding can spotlight what sets you apart.

Creating Recall: A memorable brand ensures that even if a potential customer doesn't purchase immediately, they're likely to recall your shop when they decide to make a purchase in the future.

Branding, in the realm of online sales, isn't a mere luxury—it's a necessity. It's the voice that speaks for you when you aren't there, the thread that binds your crafts, your story, and your customers. By understanding and harnessing its power, craft sellers can not only boost sales but also build lasting relationships with their audience.

Tips for Naming your Online Shop

Choosing a name for your online craft shop is akin to naming a child. Seriously. It carries the identity, embodies the essence, and sets the tone for interactions. A name, succinct yet evocative, can be a potent tool for brand recall and engagement. This section offers a comprehensive guide to ensure that your shop's name not only mirrors the soul of your craft but also resonates with your target audience.

1. Reflect Your Craft and Ethos

Embedded Meaning: A great shop name often contains subtle hints or direct references to the nature of your products or the crafting process itself. For instance, if you specialise in wooden sculptures, names like "WoodWhims" or "TimberTales" might be apt.

Resonate with Your Vision: If there's a larger vision or message behind your craft, let the name echo it. For a sustainable, eco-friendly craft brand, names like "EcoCraftique" or "GreenGlimmer" could work.

2. Keep It Simple and Memorable

Avoid Complexity: While it's tempting to be unique, avoid names that are too long, difficult to spell, or hard to pronounce. A simple name ensures easy recall and minimises errors when potential customers search for your shop.

Acronyms & Initials: Be cautious when using acronyms or initials. While they might make sense to you, they might be confusing or meaningless to potential customers.

Rhythm and Alliteration: Names that have a rhythm or employ alliteration (e.g., "CraftyCorner" or "BeadedBliss") tend to be more catchy and memorable.

3. Ensure Availability and Consistency

Domain Check: Before finalising, ensure the name is available as a domain (.com, .net, etc.). Having a matching website domain lends professionalism and makes your shop easier to find. You may not want to build a website straight away if you plan to sell on platforms like Etsy, but it's good to purchase the domain (often less than $10) and keep the option open.

Social Media Handles: Consistency across platforms aids in brand recognition. Check the availability of the name on key social media platforms like Instagram, Facebook, Pinterest, and Twitter.

Avoid Trademark Issues: Ensure your chosen name doesn't infringe on any existing trademarks. It's advisable to do a quick search on trademark databases relevant to your country.

4. Future-Proof Your Name

Avoid Being TOO Niche: If there's a possibility of expanding your craft range in the future, choose a name that doesn't limit you to a specific category or product.

Flexible for Scaling: As your brand grows, you might venture into related areas, collaborations, or even physical stores. A name that remains relevant and doesn't require rebranding is ideal.

5. Add a Personal Touch

Incorporate Your Name: Using your name or a variation can make the brand feel intimate and personalised. For instance, "Anna's Artisanal Accents" has a warm, personal touch to it.

Narrate a Story: Names that come with a backstory or a personal anecdote can be engaging and memorable. If there's a unique tale or inspiration behind your craft, let it influence your shop's name.

6. Test It Out

Feedback from Trustworthy Sources: Once you have a few names in mind, seek opinions from friends, family, or fellow crafters. They might offer a fresh perspective and highlight aspects you haven't considered.

First Impressions: Ask people what they envision when they hear the name. It's a quick way to gauge if the name aligns with the image you intend to convey.

The name of your online craft shop is more than just an identifier—it's the first brushstroke on the canvas of your brand's story. While the process might seem daunting, with careful consideration and a sprinkle of creativity, you can coin a name that stands as a testament to your passion, craft, and entrepreneurial spirit.

Design Elements: Logo, Banner, and Branding Aesthetics

Design elements, when harmonised correctly, not only enhance the visual appeal of your online store but also solidify your brand's identity. From the logo that stamps your brand's mark to the banner that greets visitors, every visual cue communicates something vital about your craft and ethos. Here's a deep dive into understanding and optimising these design elements for your online craft shop.

1. Logo Design: The Emblem of Your Craft

A logo should be simple enough for instant recognition yet carry depth in its design. Think of it as a visual haiku, short but deeply meaningful.

Color Psychology:
- Colour Choices: Colours evoke emotions. Reds convey passion, blues trust and calm, greens nature and tranquillity, and so on.
- Harmony: Choose colours that not only represent your brand but also work harmoniously together. For crafts, earthy or pastel tones often resonate well.

Typography Matters:
- Legibility: Your brand name should be easily readable in the logo, even when resized.
- Mood and Style: Different fonts convey different vibes. Serif fonts might feel traditional, while sans-serif fonts often feel modern.

Consider readability, functionality, brand voice, message and overall aesthetic.

Symbolism:
- Iconic Representation: If you're using symbols or icons, they should have a direct or abstract relation to your craft.
- Avoiding Clichés: While certain symbols might seem apt, they can be overused. A unique or abstract representation can make your logo stand out.

2. Banner: The Welcoming Canvas

Ensure that your banner images are of the highest quality to look professional and appealing.

Showcasing Your Craft:
- Hero Product: Highlighting one standout product can capture attention instantly.
- Collage: A well-designed montage can give a snapshot of the range and diversity of your products.

Consistent Branding:
- Colour Palette: The banner's colours should be in harmony with your logo and overall brand palette.
- Typography: If you're using any text, ensure the font is consistent with other brand elements.

Keep it fresh and periodically update the banner, especially during seasons, festivals, or sales.

3. Branding Aesthetics: Crafting a Unified Visual Language

Consistency Across the Board:

- Images: Product images, promotional graphics, and any other visual content should follow a similar aesthetic in terms of colours, filters, and styling.
- Packaging: If you're shipping physical products, the packaging should echo the brand's colours, logo, and design elements.
- Scalability: Ensure that your design elements, especially the logo, are clear and recognisable, whether they're on a business card or a billboard.
- Platform Compatibility: The design should be adaptable across various digital platforms, be it your online shop, social media profiles, or digital advertisements.

Design is the silent ambassador of your brand. In the realm of online crafts, where tactile experience is absent, visual aesthetics play a pivotal role in connecting with the audience. By meticulously crafting each design element, you don't just sell a product; you offer a slice of your artistic vision, ensuring that visitors leave with an imprint of your brand's essence in their minds.

Writing Compelling "About" Section

The "About" section of your online craft shop acts as a bridge, connecting your craft's soul with the hearts of your audience. It's more than a mere biography; it's a narrative, a story that shares your passion, your journey, and the essence of your creations. Crafting this section with care is paramount, and here's a detailed guide to help you do just that.

1. Start with Your "Why"

The Core Motivation: What ignited your passion for crafts? Was it a childhood hobby, a family tradition, or a serendipitous discovery? Starting with this heartfelt spark can immediately capture your readers' attention.

The Greater Vision: Beyond sales, what do you aim to achieve with your craft? Perhaps you're looking to revive a dying art form, promote sustainable crafting, or simply spread joy through handmade beauties.

2. Share Your Journey

Chronicle the Milestones: Every artist has a journey, dotted with challenges, learnings, and moments of epiphany. Share key milestones that shaped your craft and your brand.

Behind-the-Scenes Glimpses: Offering insights into your creative process, the joy of crafting a new piece, or the challenges faced can make readers feel a part of your world.

3. Showcase the Unique Aspects of Your Craft

The Art and the Artist: Describe the techniques, materials, and methods you employ. If there are unique tools or traditional methods involved, shed light on them.

Sustainability and Ethics: If your craft promotes sustainability or has ethical aspects, like cruelty-free methods or fair wages for artisans, highlight them. They can be pivotal selling points in today's conscious market.

4. Personalise with Anecdotes and Memories

Crafted Memories: Share a memorable experience or a heartfelt story related to your craft. It could be about the first product you sold, a touching feedback from a customer, or even an anecdote from a crafting workshop you attended.

Inspirations: Every artist has inspirations, be it nature, travels, or personal experiences. Sharing what inspires you can make your creations more relatable and cherished.

5. Incorporate Visual Elements

Pictures Speak Louder: Include high-quality images of your workspace, your tools, or even a candid shot of you engrossed in crafting. These visuals can make the narrative more engaging and authentic.

Videos: If feasible, adding a short video that showcases your crafting process or a tour of your studio can add a dynamic touch to your "About" section.

6. Engage and Connect

Call to Action: After sharing your story, guide the readers on their next steps. Invite them to browse your collection, sign up for a newsletter, or follow you on social media.

Contact Information: Ensure that your readers have a way to reach out. Whether it's for inquiries, collaborations, or just to share their appreciation, make the contact process seamless.

Your "About" section is the heart of your online craft shop. It's where transactions gain a human touch, and where products transform into stories. By investing time and emotion into crafting this space, you pave the way for deeper connections, turning casual visitors into loyal patrons and brand advocates.

Chapter 4: Product Photography & Description

Your product's first impression isn't made by the item itself but by its digital representation: the photos and description. How can you ensure that this digital footprint does justice to your craftsmanship? There is often a tendency to over complicate this area of creating an online store and business. Therefore I am going to keep it simple and concise. Follow these instructions and you will have a well represented product, both visually and in terms of its visibility across the web.

The Role of Images in Online Selling

Instant Appeal:
Visual Connection: A compelling image can instantly captivate potential buyers, igniting their interest in your craft.
First Impressions: Often, customers decide within seconds of seeing an image whether they're interested or not, underscoring the importance of high-quality visuals.

Building Trust:
Product Authenticity: Clear, honest images showcase the genuine quality and detail of your craft.
Multiple Angles: Displaying your product from various angles gives a comprehensive view, boosting buyer confidence.

DIY Product Photography Tips:

Lighting is Key:
Natural Light: Whenever possible, use natural light. It brings out true colours and avoids harsh shadows.
Diffused Lighting: Soften your light source with diffusers or sheer curtains to avoid glaring highlights.

Background Choices:

Neutral Backdrops: White or light-coloured backdrops keep the focus on the product.
Contextual Setup: Occasionally, place the product in a context that showcases its use or aesthetic.

Steady Shooting:
Tripods: Ensure clarity by using a tripod or a stable surface to avoid shaky images.
Focus: Ensure the product is in sharp focus, with important details clear.

Post-Processing:
Editing Tools: Use tools like Adobe Lightroom, Photoshop, or even smartphone apps to tweak brightness, contrast, and sharpness.
Cropping: Ensure the product fills a substantial portion of the frame without unnecessary space.

Writing Enticing Product Descriptions

Engaging Narratives:
Tell a Story: Every craft has a backstory. Share its inspiration, the process, or the tradition it represents.
Highlight Unique Features: Emphasise what sets your product apart, be it the material, technique, or design.

Clear Specifications:
Dimensions and Size: Provide accurate measurements, sizes, or any other quantifiable details.
Materials Used: List down the materials, especially if they're eco-friendly, organic, or of a specific quality.

Addressing Potential Queries:
Care Instructions: If your product needs special care, like hand-washing or avoiding direct sunlight, mention it.
Usability & Benefits: Describe how the product can be used and any potential benefits, be they functional or aesthetic.

Using SEO to Enhance Product Visibility

Keyword Research:
Popular Terms: Use tools like Google's Keyword Planner or Ubersuggest to find relevant keywords associated with your craft.
Long-Tail Keywords: These are specific phrases customers might search for, like "hand-painted ceramic mugs" instead of just "mugs".

Optimised Titles and Descriptions:
Incorporate Keywords: Naturally integrate your researched keywords into product titles, descriptions, and even image file names.
Avoid Keyword Stuffing: Ensure the text still reads naturally and avoid cramming in keywords, which can be off-putting and can potentially lead to search engine penalties.

Meta Descriptions & Tags:
Platform-Specific: Depending on your selling platform, there might be options for meta tags or descriptions. Fill these out diligently for enhanced searchability.

Through appealing imagery and compelling descriptions, you bring your craft to life. By enhancing it with effective SEO practices, you ensure that it reaches those who will genuinely appreciate and cherish it. Thus, the harmony of aesthetics and digital strategy is the key to online craft-selling success.

Chapter 5: Pricing Your Crafts

Pricing is one of the most critical aspects of running a successful craft business. It's a delicate balance between covering your costs, ensuring profitability, and offering value to your customers. In this chapter, we'll unravel the intricate web of pricing and help you set the right price tags for your crafts.

Calculating Cost of Materials and Time

Inventory and Supplies

Tracking Expenses:

- *Maintaining Records*: In the age of digital tools, consider using apps or software like QuickBooks, Excel, or even a simple notebook to jot down every purchase related to your craft.
- *Itemised Receipts*: Whenever you buy supplies, ensure you get detailed receipts. This makes it easier to log exact costs and aids in tax deductions related to your business.
- *Adjusting for Waste*: Recognise that not every bit of material you buy will end up in a finished product. For instance, if you're a jeweller, some metal might be lost in the crafting process. Factor in these "waste" costs to get a true sense of material expenses.

Bulk Purchasing:

- *Cost-Benefit Analysis*: This sounds more complex than it is. Buying in bulk often results in a cheaper unit price. However, do a cost-benefit analysis factoring in potential waste, storage costs, and the risk of materials becoming obsolete or outdated.
- *Storage Solutions*: Invest in proper storage solutions to ensure the longevity of your materials. For example, if you're into organic crafting, some materials might need temperature-controlled environments.

- *Supplier Relations*: Building a good rapport with suppliers can lead to discounts, better quality materials, or first access to new stock.

<u>Time is Money</u>

Hourly Rate:

- *Understanding Your Worth*: Your craft might be your passion, but turning it into a business means recognizing the economic value of your skills. What would you reasonably pay someone with your skillset to do the same work?
- *Overhead Costs*: Apart from direct material costs, factor in overheads such as utilities, rent (if you rent a studio space), software subscriptions, etc. These should be divided over the number of items you produce in a given period to determine their contribution to the hourly rate.
- *Profit Margin*: Your hourly rate should also leave room for profit. After all, this isn't just about breaking even but growing a sustainable business.

Production Time:

- *Time Tracking*: Start tracking the time you spend on each item, from conception to final touches. Tools like Toggl or even a simple stopwatch can help.
- *Scaling Considerations*: Recognize that as you produce more, you might become more efficient and reduce production time. Regularly revisit and adjust your time calculations accordingly.
- *Intangible Aspects*: Crafting isn't just physical labour. The time spent brainstorming, researching, or even correcting mistakes counts. Make sure these hours are also factored into your overall production time.

Understanding the true cost of your craft involves more than just tallying up receipts. It's a holistic understanding of both tangible expenses and the intangible value of your time and expertise. By meticulously calculating these, you set a firm foundation for pricing that ensures both sustainability and growth for your crafting business.

Understanding Market Value

<u>Research Competitors</u>

Price Range:

- *Comprehensive Market Scan*: Start by browsing popular online marketplaces, craft fairs, or stores that cater to your niche. This will give you a range of prices and a better understanding of what customers might expect to pay.
- *Segmentation*: Not all crafts in your niche will be at the same quality or price level. Identify if there are different segments (e.g., luxury, mid-range, budget) and determine where your crafts fit.
- *Adjusting for Geography*: Consider that prices might vary based on location. If a particular craft is rare in one region but common in another, this could impact its market value.

Value Proposition:

- *Unique Selling Points (USP)*: Identify and articulate what's unique about your craft. It could be the technique, materials, story behind it, or even your personal brand.
- *Emotional Connection*: Often, crafts aren't just objects; they carry stories, emotions, or memories. If your craft offers such an emotional connection, it could be a significant value addition.
- *Perceived Value*: Sometimes, the value isn't just in the tangible product but in the intangibles like exclusivity, a limited edition, or being hand-made. Understand the perception of value from a customer's perspective.

Understanding market value goes beyond merely matching the price tag of competitors. It's a nuanced process of recognising the tangible and intangible aspects that dictate a craft's value. By constantly staying attuned to market trends and feedback, you ensure that your pricing is dynamic, competitive, and reflective of genuine market demand.

Offering Deals and Discounts

Strategic offers help to make your customers feel valued and in turn like they are getting value for money. It also helps drive momentum for your business and momentum is key.

Launch Offers:
- *Driving Initial Sales*: When you release a new product, an introductory discount can pique interest and incentivize customers to make a purchase, even if they're initially hesitant.
- *Gathering Early Reviews*: A new product with reviews is more trustworthy to potential customers. Offering a launch discount can accelerate the process of getting those crucial first reviews.
- *Market Feedback*: Early bird discounts can also provide an opportunity to gather feedback on the new product. Use this intel to make any adjustments before the product becomes widely popular.

Seasonal Promotions:
- *Calendar-Based Discounts*: Align your discount strategy with major holidays (e.g., Christmas, Valentine's Day) or events relevant to your craft (like National Craft Month).
- *Clearance Sales*: If you work with materials or designs that are season-specific (like winter-themed crafts), end-of-season sales can help clear out stock and make room for new designs.
- *Flash Sales*: Occasionally, short-term, significant discounts (like a 24-hour sale) can create urgency and drive sales, especially when combined with effective marketing strategies.

Loyalty Programs

Again, loyalty programs are a great way to retain customers especially when executed in line with branding initiatives and your company values. It's not just about making your customers aware of your journey, but about bring them along on it.

Rewards for Repeat Purchases:

- *Point-Based Systems*: For every purchase, customers earn points which can be redeemed later. This not only encourages repeat purchases but also can drive larger order values.
- *Tiered Loyalty Programs*: The more a customer shops, the higher they climb in loyalty tiers, unlocking more significant benefits. This can motivate customers to reach the next tier by shopping more frequently.
- *Exclusive Access*: Offer loyal customers early access to new products, special editions, or limited stock items as a part of the loyalty program.

Referral Bonuses:

- *Win-Win Offers*: Design a referral program where both the referrer and the referee get benefits. For instance, if a customer refers a friend, both might get a 10% discount on their next purchase.
- *Easy Sharing*: Incorporate easy sharing options on your website or platform. QR codes, referral links, or share buttons can make the referral process seamless.
- *Tracking and Redemption*: Ensure that your system effectively tracks referrals and makes the redemption process straightforward. This will prevent any potential frustrations and disputes.

Deals and discounts aren't just about reducing prices. They're strategic tools that, when used wisely, can boost sales, encourage customer loyalty, and provide valuable feedback. The key is to strike a balance – offering perks to attract and retain customers while ensuring the business remains profitable. By understanding the purpose behind each discount and structuring them effectively, you can foster a loyal customer base and enhance their brand's appeal.

Shipping and Handling Considerations

It's important to understand your packaging costs and any risks of transit. No need to overcomplicate it, but neglecting this area can soon eat into your profits and dampen the experience of your customers.

Protective Packaging:

Balancing Safety and Cost: While it's paramount to ensure items reach customers in pristine condition, there's a fine line between adequate protection and over-packaging. Assess the fragility of your craft items and find the most cost-effective solution that ensures safety.

Eco-Friendly Options: With growing concern for the environment, consider using recyclable or biodegradable packaging. Not only can this sometimes be cost-effective, but it can also be a selling point for environmentally-conscious customers.

Customised Solutions: Sometimes, specialised packaging (like jewellery boxes or fabric pouches) can serve as both protection and an added value for the customer.

Branding:

Enhanced Unboxing Experience: A beautifully branded package can turn the unboxing experience into a memorable moment, encouraging repeat purchases and word-of-mouth marketing.

Cost-Benefit Analysis: While branded packaging can be more costly, consider its potential return in terms of customer loyalty, brand recall, and potential social media shares.

Stickers and Stamps: If custom boxes are beyond your budget, consider branded stickers, stamps, or thank-you cards as an affordable way to infuse branding into the packaging.

Shipping Rates:

- *Simplicity vs. Accuracy*: A fixed shipping rate is simple and straightforward for customers, but may sometimes mean you overcharge or undercharge. Variable rates can be more accurate but might require customers to input more information, potentially slowing down the checkout process.
- *Free Shipping Strategy*: Offering free shipping can be a significant sales driver. If opting for this, ensure the product price adequately covers the shipping cost. Highlighting "free shipping" in promotions can also attract more buyers.

Processing Time:

- *Set Realistic Expectations*: Clearly indicate the expected time between order placement and dispatch. This helps manage customer expectations and prevent dissatisfaction.
- *Factors to Consider*: Your processing time may vary based on the nature of the craft (made-to-order vs. ready-to-ship), the volume of orders you receive, and any personal or seasonal factors.

Rush Orders:

- *Feasibility*: Before offering expedited processing, ensure you can consistently meet the quicker turnaround without compromising on craft quality.
- *Pricing*: Consider the additional stress, potential for error, or need for overtime when pricing rush orders. The fee should cover these extra costs and potential risks.

Shipping and handling are often the final touchpoints of an online sale but can make or break the customer experience. By balancing costs, ensuring reliability, and providing clear communication, craft sellers can enhance customer satisfaction and foster trust. As e-commerce continues to grow, mastering these logistical aspects will be pivotal for any online craft business.

Chapter 6: Marketing and Promotion

Leveraging Social Media

Visual Showcase: Use Instagram as a visual portfolio, showcasing high-quality images and videos of your crafts.
Stories & Reels: Engage your audience with behind-the-scenes content, promotions, and interactive polls or questions.
Hashtags: Research and use relevant hashtags to increase the discoverability of your posts.

Community Building: Create a Facebook page or group to build a community around your craft brand. Engage with customers, share updates, and seek feedback.
Facebook Shop: Integrate a shop into your Facebook page, allowing users to browse and buy without leaving the platform.
Live Sessions: Host live crafting sessions or product launches to engage with your audience in real-time.

Craft Inspiration: Pinterest is a haven for craft enthusiasts. Create pins that not only showcase your products but also provide inspiration to potential buyers.
Tutorial Pins: Consider creating step-by-step pins or infographics that give a sneak peek into your crafting process.
Shop the Look: Utilise Pinterest's shopping features to direct users straight from a pin to a purchase.

Email Marketing and Building a Subscriber List

Once you have a customer, using email to keep engagement open is a great way to secure future sales and repeat custom. Extending that community feel and making them part of your journey goes a seriously long way. Some methods include:

- *Subscription Incentives*: Offer discounts or exclusive content as an incentive for visitors to subscribe to your newsletter.
- Regular Updates: Send out newsletters showcasing new products, sharing company news, or offering special deals.
- *Segmentation*: As your list grows, segment your subscribers based on purchase history or interests to send targeted emails, increasing engagement and conversions.
- *Automated Campaigns*: Use tools to set up automated campaigns like abandoned cart reminders or post-purchase thank-you emails.

Collaborations and partnerships can extend this further once you get more comfortable with your online presence and engagement:

- *Craft Bloggers & Influencers*: Collaborate with bloggers or social media influencers in the craft space for product reviews or giveaways.
- *Joint Promotions*: Partner with non-competing craft businesses to run joint promotions, expanding your reach to a new audience.
- *Craft Fairs & Events*: Participate in or sponsor craft fairs. Collaborate with organisers for special promotions or workshops.

Paid Advertising: Basics and Best Platforms for Craft Products

Paid ads are also a great way to boost sales but the costs can soon rack up if not well planned. Targeted ads on the right platform can be extremely powerful and once you reach a certain point with your product, branding and supply, you will want to look into this.

- *Understanding Ad Platforms*: Each platform, from Google Ads to Facebook Ads, has its unique features. Understand where your target audience spends their time.
- *Setting a Budget*: Determine an advertising budget. Start small, test different ad types and platforms, then scale what works.
- *Craft-Centric Platforms*: Platforms like Pinterest or Etsy Ads are particularly beneficial for craft businesses. These platforms already have an audience interested in handmade and unique products.
- *Ad Creatives*: Ensure your advertisements are visually appealing, with clear product images and compelling call-to-actions.

Marketing and promotion are crucial in turning a craft hobby into a thriving online business. The digital age offers numerous tools and platforms to reach potential customers worldwide. By understanding each tool's strengths and strategically investing time and resources, craft entrepreneurs can build a loyal customer base and achieve lasting business success.

Chapter 7: Customer Relations & Feedback

Your products are vital. There is no doubt about that. But the experience and interactions you offer can make or break your venture. The way you engage with your customers and the value you place on their feedback are what can set you apart in a large marketplace. This can be yet another opportunity to showcase your brands character and ethos, resulting in loyal patrons and brand champions.

Importance of Customer Reviews

JA Jayme
3 reviews © GB

★★★★★ ✓ Verified   Oct 5, 2021

Received my personalised wove bracelet...

Received my personalised wove bracelet in speedy time and absolutely love it! Exactly what I wanted and quality is great! Will definitely recommend and more than likely purchase again!

Date of experience: October 05, 2021

👍 Useful   ⤳ Share   ⚑

Building Trust:
- *Authenticity and Credibility*: Potential customers often rely on reviews to gauge the reliability and quality of a product. Authentic positive reviews can significantly enhance trust.
- *SEO and Visibility*: Positive reviews can improve search engine rankings, especially on platforms like Etsy and Amazon Handmade.

Social Proof:
- *Increased Conversion Rates*: Products with a higher number of positive reviews tend to have better conversion rates, as they reduce the perceived risk for a potential buyer.

- *Informed Decisions*: Detailed reviews can provide additional information or address concerns not covered in the product description.

Soliciting Reviews:
- *Post-Purchase Emails*: Send a gentle reminder to customers requesting a review after their purchase.
- *Incentives*: Offer small discounts or bonus items in return for leaving a review.

Handling Customer Complaints and Returns:

It's important to be consistent and objective in your approach to resolving complaints. An example process is as follows:

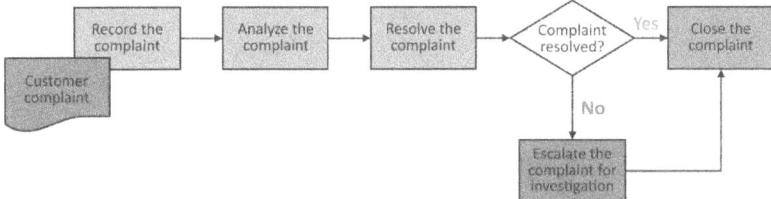

Steps for handling the complaint

It may seem simple, but having something on paper can help you ensure you follow the rights steps every time without getting disheartened.

Proactive Communication:
- *Clear Policies*: Ensure your return and exchange policies are clear, fair, and visible on your online store.
- *Open Channels*: Allow customers to easily reach out through various channels, including email, chat, or social media.

Empathy and Understanding:
- *Listen Actively*: Ensure the customer feels heard, and genuinely listen to their concerns.

- *Quick Responses*: Aim to address complaints swiftly, reducing the customer's frustration.

Solutions-Oriented Approach:
- *Flexible Policies*: While it's essential to have return policies, be prepared to make exceptions to enhance customer satisfaction occasionally.
- *Follow-Up*: After resolving a complaint, follow up with the customer to ensure they're satisfied with the solution.

Using Feedback to Improve

Constructive Criticism:
- *Continuous Learning*: Embrace negative feedback as an opportunity to refine your products or services.
- *Engage with Feedback*: Respond to reviews, both positive and negative, showing customers you value their input.

Feedback Analysis:
- *Trends and Patterns*: Look for recurring feedback themes to identify areas of improvement.
- *Product Development*: Use feedback to inspire new product ideas or enhancements.

Encouraging Repeat Business and Loyalty

Loyalty Programs:
- *Points System*: Offer points for every purchase, which can be redeemed for discounts or free items.
- *Exclusive Offers*: Give loyal customers access to exclusive sales, products, or content.

Engaging Content:
- *Newsletters*: Regularly update your customers about new products, company news, or crafting tips.
- *Personal Touch*: Personalise communication, like sending birthday discounts or celebrating a customer's anniversary with your store.

Value Addition:
- *More than Just Sales*: Offer value beyond products. This could be in the form of tutorials, workshops, or crafting resources.
- *Customer Appreciation*: Occasionally send a handwritten thank-you note or a small freebie with purchases to show appreciation.

Customer relations go beyond making a sale. It's about building lasting relationships, garnering trust, and fostering loyalty. A happy customer doesn't just return for more purchases but can also turn into a brand ambassador, spreading the word and bringing in more potential customers. By valuing feedback, handling complaints gracefully, and continually striving to offer value, craft entrepreneurs can ensure sustained success and growth.

Chapter 8: Expanding Your Reach

As your craft business solidifies its presence online, there's an inherent desire and logic to extend beyond the foundational platforms. The world of the internet offers myriad avenues to not only sell your products but to also establish yourself as an authority in the craft domain. By diversifying your online presence and participating in a wider array of activities, you can tap into new audiences, create additional revenue streams, and further your brand's resonance. Let's delve into some effective strategies to expand your reach.

Participating in Online Craft Fairs and Events

Virtual Craft Fairs:
- *Overview*: With the digital age and especially post-pandemic, many craft fairs have moved online. These are virtual spaces where crafters can showcase their products to a wide audience.
- *How to Participate*: Understand the technical prerequisites, such as creating virtual booths, hosting live demos, or engaging in Q&A sessions.
- *Benefits*: Access to a wider audience, reduced overhead costs compared to physical fairs, and opportunities for networking.

Webinars and Workshops:
- Host or participate in online workshops, teaching craft techniques, or discussing industry trends.
- Use platforms like Zoom, WebEx, or Google Meet to interact with attendees, making sessions engaging with polls, Q&A, and live demos.

Collaborative Projects with Other Crafters

Joint Ventures:
- *Overview*: Partner with fellow crafters to create limited-edition products, bringing together unique skills from both parties.
- *Examples*: A potter and painter collaborating on hand-painted ceramics, or a jewellery maker and textile artist creating embroidered jewellery pieces.

Guest Crafting:
- Feature on another crafter's platform or invite them onto yours, showcasing a joint crafting session or product discussion.
- Benefits: Cross-promotion to each other's audience, combined skills leading to innovative products, and shared marketing efforts.

Branching into Digital Products or Tutorials

Digital Products:
- Overview: Sell digital versions of your craft, like printable art, digital planners, or design templates.
- Benefits: No shipping hassles, passive income potential, and a broader international audience.

Paid Tutorials:
- Offer in-depth, paid tutorials for those wanting to learn your craft techniques.
- Platforms to Consider: Udemy, Skillshare, or your website.

Starting a Blog or YouTube Channel to Showcase Your Craft

Blogging:
- *Overview*: Share crafting tips, industry insights, product launches, and customer stories.
- *Benefits*: Boosts SEO, establishes authority in your niche, and offers potential for ad revenue.

YouTube:

- *Overview*: Videos can capture the crafting process, tutorials, product reviews, and more.
- *Monetisation*: Ad revenue, sponsored content, and affiliate marketing.
- *Engaging with Audience*: Use these platforms to directly engage with followers, conduct polls, gather feedback, and foster community.

Expanding your reach online is about blending creativity with strategy. As a craft entrepreneur, the digital world offers boundless opportunities to grow, not just in sales, but as a brand and an authority in your domain. Embrace these avenues, experiment, and find what aligns best with your passion and business goals. The horizon is vast; it's all about charting the course that resonates with your vision.

Chapter 9: Managing Finances

Stepping into the realm of online craft selling is not only about showcasing your creativity but also about effectively managing the financial side of your business. Like the delicate stitches of embroidery or the precise measurements in woodworking, handling finances requires attention to detail. This chapter aims to shed light on the financial nuances of running an online craft business, from the basics to tools and taxation, ensuring you have a sturdy foundation for future growth.

Basics of Online Business Finance

Revenue: This is the total income from sales before any expenses are deducted. It's essential to have a clear record of all transactions.

Expenses: These can be both fixed (like platform subscription fees or rented workspace costs) and variable (like materials or shipping costs).

Profit and Loss: By subtracting your total expenses from your revenue, you get either a profit (if positive) or a loss (if negative).

Cash Flow: This is a record of the money coming in and going out, crucial to ensure you have enough liquidity for business operations.

Tools for Tracking Sales and Expenses

Accounting Software:
Examples: QuickBooks, FreshBooks, or Zoho Books tailored for small businesses.
Features: Automated invoice creation, sales tracking, expense logging, and financial report generation.

Spreadsheet Applications:

Tools like Microsoft Excel or Google Sheets can be customised to track finances if you're not ready for dedicated accounting software.

Mobile Applications:

Apps like Evernote can be used to photograph and catalogue receipts, while Mint or YNAB can assist with budgeting.

Taxes for Online Sellers

Income Tax: As an online seller, your profits are subject to income tax. It's crucial to separate personal and business finances to calculate this accurately.

Sales Tax: Depending on your location and where you're selling, you might be required to collect sales tax from buyers.

International Sales: If selling internationally, be aware of taxes and duties applicable in the buyer's country.

Deductions: Familiarise yourself with potential tax deductions available to online businesses, such as home office deductions or expenses related to advertising.

Professional Guidance: Consider consulting with an accountant familiar with online businesses to ensure compliance and optimise deductions.

Planning for Future Growth

Reinvesting Profits: Consider putting a portion of your profits back into the business, whether for marketing, new tools, or expanding your product line.

Setting Financial Goals: Determine clear, actionable financial goals. For instance, aim for a specific revenue target or set aside a budget for an upcoming marketing campaign.

Financial Contingencies: It's wise to have a financial safety net. Set aside a portion of earnings for unforeseen business expenses or slow sales periods.

Scaling Operations: As you grow, you might need to hire help, invest in larger workspaces, or use more advanced tools. Plan and budget for these potential future needs.

Managing finances might seem daunting, especially if you ventured into online craft selling primarily driven by passion. However, with the right tools, knowledge, and perhaps a little professional guidance, you can navigate this aspect with confidence. By keeping a meticulous record, understanding taxes, and planning for the future, you ensure your craft business isn't just artistically rewarding but financially sustainable and prosperous too.

Chapter 10: Staying Inspired & Adapting to Trends

In the dynamic world of online craft selling, where creativity meets business, staying inspired and relevant is paramount. While your craft began as a passion, the continuous churn of the marketplace can sometimes dull the spark. The key is to evolve while holding onto the essence of what made you start crafting in the first place. This chapter dives into the delicate dance of preserving authenticity while being adaptable to ever-changing trends.

Continuously Learning and Evolving

Educational Opportunities
- Consider enrolling in online courses or workshops related to your craft or business skills.
- Stay updated with books and magazines dedicated to crafts, design, and entrepreneurship.

Experimentation:
- Dedicate time to just "play" with your craft without the pressure of selling, allowing for organic creativity.
- Explore new materials, techniques, or styles to refresh your perspective and product line.

Joining Online Craft Communities for Support and Inspiration

Forums & Discussion Boards: Websites like Craftster or Ravelry can be goldmines for sharing ideas, asking questions, and getting feedback.

Social Media Groups: Platforms like Facebook have numerous craft-specific groups where members share their creations, techniques, and advice.

Virtual Workshops and Webinars: Engaging in virtual events can expose you to new techniques and trends while networking with fellow crafters.

Keeping an Eye on Market Trends

Trend Analysis Tools: Use platforms like Pinterest or Etsy's Trend Report to spot emerging trends in the craft world.

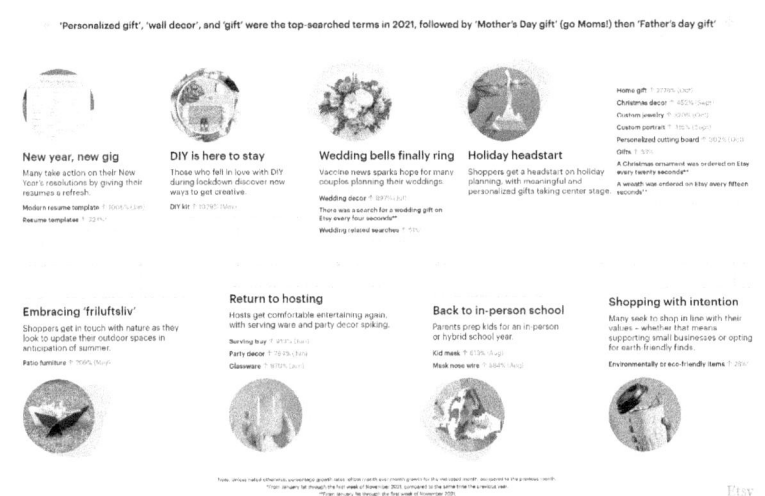

'Personalized gift', 'wall decor', and 'gift' were the top-searched terms in 2021, followed by 'Mother's Day gift' (go Moms!) then 'Father's day gift'

Fashion & Design Shows: Even if not directly related to your craft, these events often set the tone for colours, patterns, and styles for the upcoming seasons.

Customer Feedback: Regularly solicit feedback from your buyers. They can offer valuable insights into what's becoming popular or going out of style.

Balancing Authenticity with Adaptability

Stay True to Your Craft: While it's beneficial to adapt to trends, it's crucial to retain the essence of your work. Don't lose what makes your craft uniquely yours.

Evolving without Losing Identity: If neon colours are trending but your craft revolves around earthy tones, think of ways to introduce hints of neon without a complete overhaul. Adaptation should feel organic, not forced.

Listening to Your Inner Creator: Sometimes, trends won't resonate with you, and that's okay. Your genuine passion will shine through in your work, drawing customers who appreciate authenticity.

It's easy to feel overwhelmed by the rapid pace of change. However, the core of your craft business is your unique perspective and creativity. By continually learning, engaging with a supportive community, keeping an eye on market trends, and balancing adaptability with authenticity, you ensure your craft remains both relevant and true to its roots. Remember, trends come and go, but the passion and authenticity behind genuine craftsmanship always stand out.

Conclusion

The odyssey of transforming a deeply ingrained passion into a profitable venture is truly commendable. Embarking on such a journey requires not just immense skill and creativity, but also resilience, adaptability, and an undying enthusiasm to continuously evolve. By choosing to monetise your craft, you've bridged the world of artistry and commerce, making your beloved hobby accessible and cherished by many.

Throughout this guide, we've journeyed together through the intricate nuances of setting up, branding, marketing, and continuously refining your craft business. But it's essential to understand that this guide is merely a foundation, a starting point. The world of online craft selling is vibrant and constantly changing. With each passing trend, there are lessons to learn, new strategies to adopt, and innovative techniques to master.

But beyond all the business strategies and techniques, it's vital to stay connected to the core of your craft – your passion. It's the wellspring of creativity and the very essence that sets your products apart. Never lose sight of that initial spark, the love for crafting that got you started on this path. Embrace challenges as they come, view them as opportunities to grow, and never hesitate to seek inspiration from the vast reservoir of global craft communities.

As we wrap up this guide, remember that every day presents a new learning opportunity. Continuous growth, both as an artist and an entrepreneur, is the key to success in the dynamic online marketplace. To further assist you on your journey, consider exploring additional resources, attending workshops, or joining craft communities to stay updated and inspired.

To all the crafters reading this – your passion, dedication, and creativity are commendable. Here's to turning dreams into tangible art, and art into a successful business. Wishing you every success on this beautiful, craft-filled journey. Cheers!